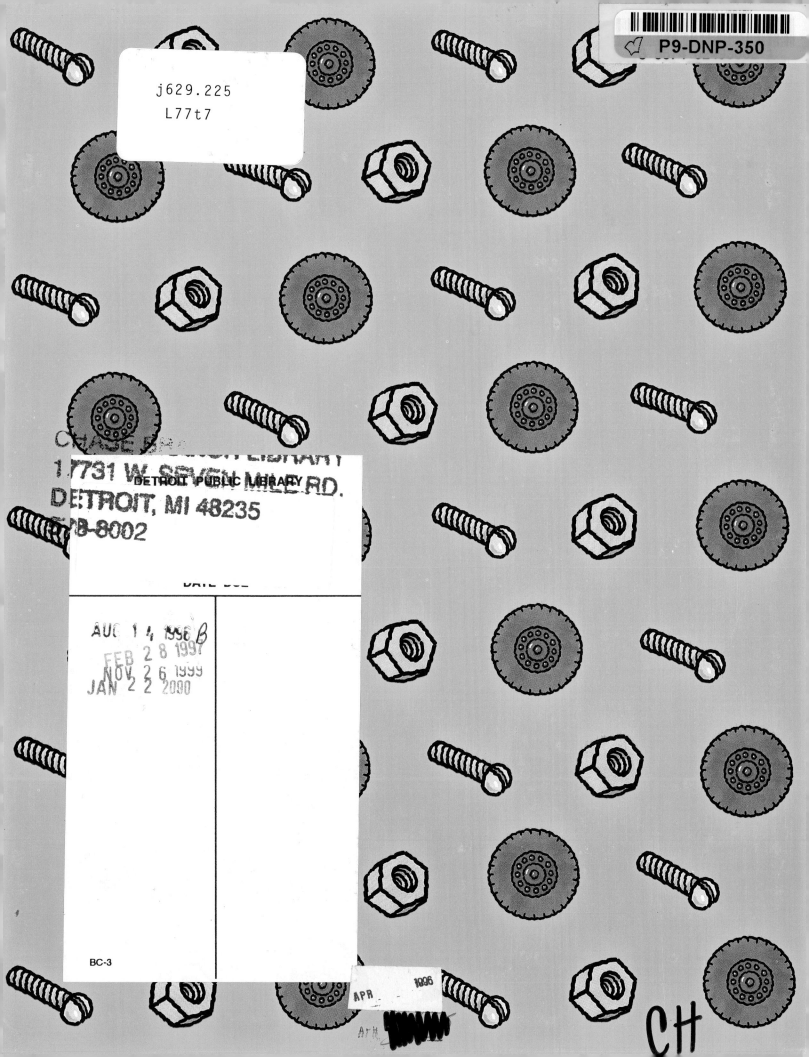

CH

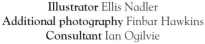

A DORLING KINDERSLEY BOOK

Editor Miriam Farbey
Designer Helen Melville
Managing Editor Sheila Hanly
US Editor Camela Decaire
Production Catherine Semark
Photography Mike Dunning,
Richard Leeney
Illustrator Ellis Nadler
Additional photography Finbar Hawkins
Consultant Ian Ogilvie

First American Edition, 1995
2 4 6 8 10 9 7 5 3 1

Published in the United States by
Dorling Kindersley Publishing, Inc.,
95 Madison Avenue, New York, New York 10016

Library of Congress Cataloging-in-Publication Data

Llewellyn, Claire.
    Truck / Claire Llewellyn. — 1st American ed.
        p.   cm.
    ISBN 1-56458-516-6
    1. Trucks—Juvenile literature.   2. Earthmoving
machinery—Juvenile literature.   [1. Trucks.
2. Earthmoving machinery.]
I. Title.
TL230.15.L58   1995
629.224—dc20   94–38034
                                                    CIP
                                                    AC

Color reproduction by Chromagraphics, Singapore
Printed and bound in Italy by L.E.G.O.

Dorling Kindersley would like to thank Miller Mining
for their help in producing this book.

The publisher would like to thank the following
for their kind permission to reproduce photographs:
Caterpillar Inc.: 19 top Terex Equipment Ltd.:
4 bottom left, 15 top right, 18 top

Scale

Look out for drawings
like this – they show
the size of the machines
compared with people.

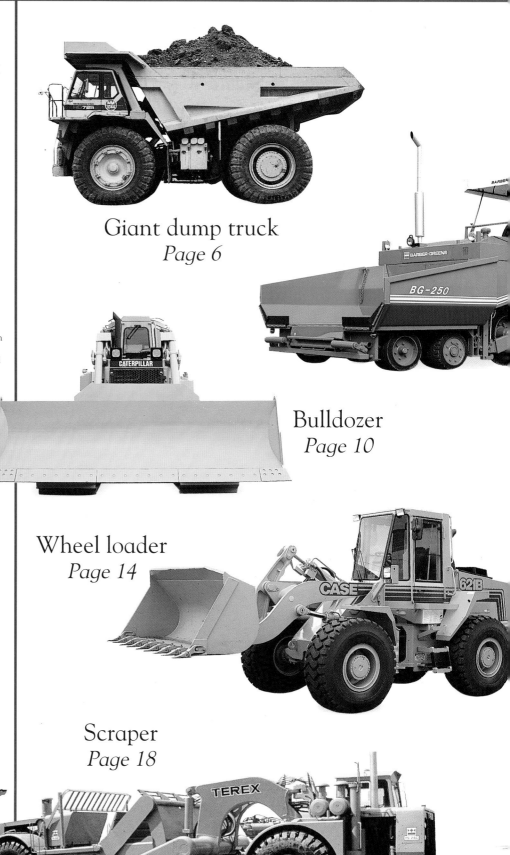

Giant dump truck

Bulldozer

Wheel loader

Scraper

Paver
Page 20

Mighty Machines

TRUCK

Claire Llewellyn

Mass excavator
Page 8

Backhoe loader
Page 12

Forklift
Page 16

DK

DORLING KINDERSLEY
LONDON • NEW YORK • STUTTGART

Giant dump truck

A giant dump truck works on the biggest building jobs or in quarries and mines. It carries enormous loads of earth and rock in its body, then tips them out wherever they are needed.

dumper body

Scale

AMAZING FACTS

The truck is 54 feet (5 meters) tall. Two adults standing one on top of the other can't reach the top.

The dumper body can hold up to 100 tons (90 tonnes) of earth – that's as heavy as 18 elephants.

sturdy steel ladder

The **body** is made of thick steel. The driver climbs a **ladder** to reach the cab.

driver sits
in the cab

Tipping out
Sliding arms, called pistons,
lift the body into the air,
and the load slides out
with a crash!

heaped
load of
earth

KOMATSU HD 785 MM 1044

The **cab** contains the steering wheel, levers, and pedals that control the machine.

Mass excavator

A mass excavator is a huge digging machine. It has a long arm with a bucket attached to the end. The bucket scoops up soil or rock and empties it into a dump truck. Different-sized buckets, as well as attachments such as hammers, can be fixed to the arm.

jointed arm

sharp teeth bite deep into soil

bucket splits open to empty a load

platform swivels around so the arm can work in every direction

Attachments are tools fixed to a machine. **A jointed arm** bends like your arm.

pistons push out the arm

machine crawls on metal tracks

Track excavator

This excavator is only half the size of a mass excavator. It is used on smaller building sites to dig trenches for pipes, drains, and electric cables.

320 L CAT

O&K

MM708

AMAZING FACTS

A hammer attachment can pound concrete 1,400 times a minute – 20 times faster than you could.

A grapple attachment has claws for picking up scrap, or bits of metal.

With the arm stretched right out, the machine is 65 feet (20 meters) long – that's almost as long as a tennis court.

Scale

Metal tracks help machines move smoothly over bumps and grip soft ground.

Bulldozer

This powerful earthmover has a large metal blade that pushes piles of soil, bricks, or rubble out of the way. The blade's sharp cutting edge cuts through anything in its path. Bulldozing leaves land clear and flat – ready for building on.

Ripping stuff
Some bulldozers have a ripper attachment made of metal spikes at the back. This tears up stony ground as the bulldozer drives along.

curved blade

CATERPILLAR

CAT

TOTAL PRODUCT SUPPORT SERVICES

cutting edge

All cut up
The blade's razor-sharp cutting edge can slice through broad tree trunks.

Diesel fuel is an oily liquid that can be burned in a vehicle to make it go.

arms tilt
the blade

Up and down
The blade can tilt
downward to cut and
push, or upward to
pile up a load of earth.

tank holds
diesel fuel

D6H LGP

strong steel
frame

A bulldozer moves
as much soil in 3 minutes
as you could shovel in
one day.

A bulldozer weighs
20 tons (18 tonnes) –
that's as heavy as 700
seven-year-old children.

In a tug-of-war, one
bulldozer can beat at
least 250 people.

A bulldozer uses
90 gallons (337 liters)
of diesel fuel in a day –
that would probably
last a car for a month.

Scale

Steel is a hard, tough metal made from iron and the element carbon.

Backhoe loader

AMAZING FACTS

⚙ The smallest bucket is 6 inches (15 centimeters) wide – not big enough to catch a beachball.

⚙ The arm can reach to the bottom of rivers 20 feet (6 meters) deep – that's 20 times deeper than your bathtub.

A backhoe loader is two machines in one. At the front is a big shovel for loading up and carrying earth. At the back is a long, powerful arm. Different buckets can be attached to the arm to scoop out trenches for pipes or dig holes for house foundations.

Scale

mirror

exhaust pipe

powerful pistons lift the shovel high into the air

⚙ Waste steam and gas are forced out of the engine through the **exhaust pipe**.

Front action

The shovel's sharp edge levels earth like a bulldozer.

cutting edge

Toothy bucket

Back buckets have metal teeth. These help crunch through the ground to dig deep ditches.

3CX

JCB

arm reaches up, down, and from side to side

driver's seat swivels to face the front or back of the cab

bucket tilts to empty its load

feet called stabilizers keep the machine steady while it is digging

Truck drivers use **mirrors** to look all around them – even behind them. 13

Wheel loader

AMAZING FACTS

A wheel loader is an all-around shoveling, lifting, and loading machine. It works in a lot of places: loading logs onto trucks in a forest, moving sand, gravel, and soil on a building site, or unloading ships at docks.

Some wheel loaders bend in the middle – this helps them turn in small spaces.

The bucket can hold 9 tons (8 tonnes) of sand. You could build 6,000 big sand castles with that much sand.

Scale

bucket with sharp teeth cuts into rock

arms lift the bucket

A wheel loader weighs over 12 tons (11 tonnes) – that's as heavy as a bus full of children.

big tires help the loader roll smoothly over bumps

14   A **tire** is a rubber ring that is fitted around a wheel and filled with air.

Giant wheel loader

This machine is almost ten times bigger than other wheel loaders. It digs out massive chunks of rock in a quarry.

heavy chunk of rock

thick glass helps keep the cab quiet

621B

Wood pile
A log grapple can be attached to the loader for stacking logs.

Spill proof
Try to run with a bucket of water. Don't spill any! Loaders carry buckets without spilling a stone.

ladder has rails at the top to help the driver climb safely

DANGER

Stone, slate, or marble for building is cut from the Earth's surface in a **quarry**.

Moving machines

AMAZING FACTS

A site dumper's skip swivels around so it can tip its load out to the left or right.

On bumpy ground, a forklift's mast tilts back and forth to balance the load so it doesn't slide off.

Forklifts raise pallets 23 feet (7 meters) high – as high as a two-story building.

Scale

Forklift

You can see forklift trucks on building sites or in the warehouse of your local supermarket. Their prongs, or forks, slide into wooden pallets loaded with goods. The pallets are then lifted up the truck's mast and carried wherever they are needed.

— mast

long prongs

A **pallet** is a wooden tray with holes through the sides for a forklift's prongs.

arms reach over the cab so the bucket can dig in front of the machine

bucket attachment

headlight is turned on for night work

Clean sweep
A broom fixed to a skid steer sweeps up to 10 times faster than you can.

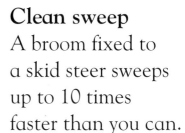

Skid steer
A small skid steer zips around a building site digging, loading, or cutting with its bucket, pallet fork, or blade attachments.

Site dumper
This little dump truck reaches only halfway up a giant dump truck's wheel. But it can carry loads that are twice its own weight.

safety bar protects the driver if the dumper rolls over

skip tilts for dumping

A **headlight** shines light on the road ahead.   A **skip** is a large, open container.

Road builders

Scraper

A scraper clears the path for a new road. It slices through hills and forests with its sharp blade.

Scale

scraper bowl collects loose earth

Grader

The metal blade of a grader scrapes the top, bumpy layer off the ground. It makes the ground smooth and level, ready for a road to be laid on it.

Scale

engine

cutting blade

18   An **engine** turns heat from burning fuel into energy to make a vehicle move.

Scale

spikes crush
extra-hard
earth

Compactor

A compactor has heavy drums with fearsome spikes that press on the ground to make a firm bed for a road. Compactors often flatten garbage at a dump.

shovel levels
the ground

drum

Scale

Articulated dump truck

This truck carries crushed stones to be laid on flattened ground. The body lifts up so that the load slides out. The truck also bends in the middle so it can turn around in tight places.

dumper body

2566B

TEREX

An **articulated** vehicle is made of two parts so it can bend in the middle.

Paver and roller

Paver

A paver lays the final surface on new roads. Hot tar and small stones are loaded into its hopper. They pass through the machine and out the back to be spread by a blade called a screed.

canopy protects the driver from the sun

iron screed

hopper

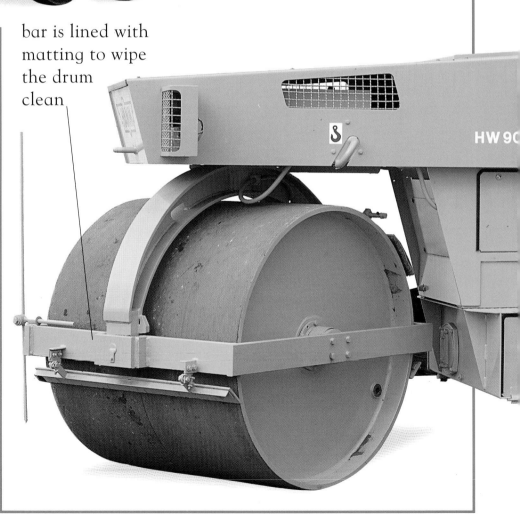

bar is lined with matting to wipe the drum clean

Busybody

One hopperful of tar and stones covers only 16 feet (5 meters) of road. It takes 12 trucks to load the hopper with enough material to keep the paver busy.

A **hopper** is a square box with a hole at the bottom through which materials pass.

Roller

A roller drives behind the road paver. It has three massive wheels, called drums, filled with water to make them heavy. The drums press down on the new road surface until it is smooth and flat. Water is sprayed over the drums to cool the hot pavement so it sets and hardens.

steel drum

plug

When the **plug** is pulled out, water flows out of the drum through the plughole. 21

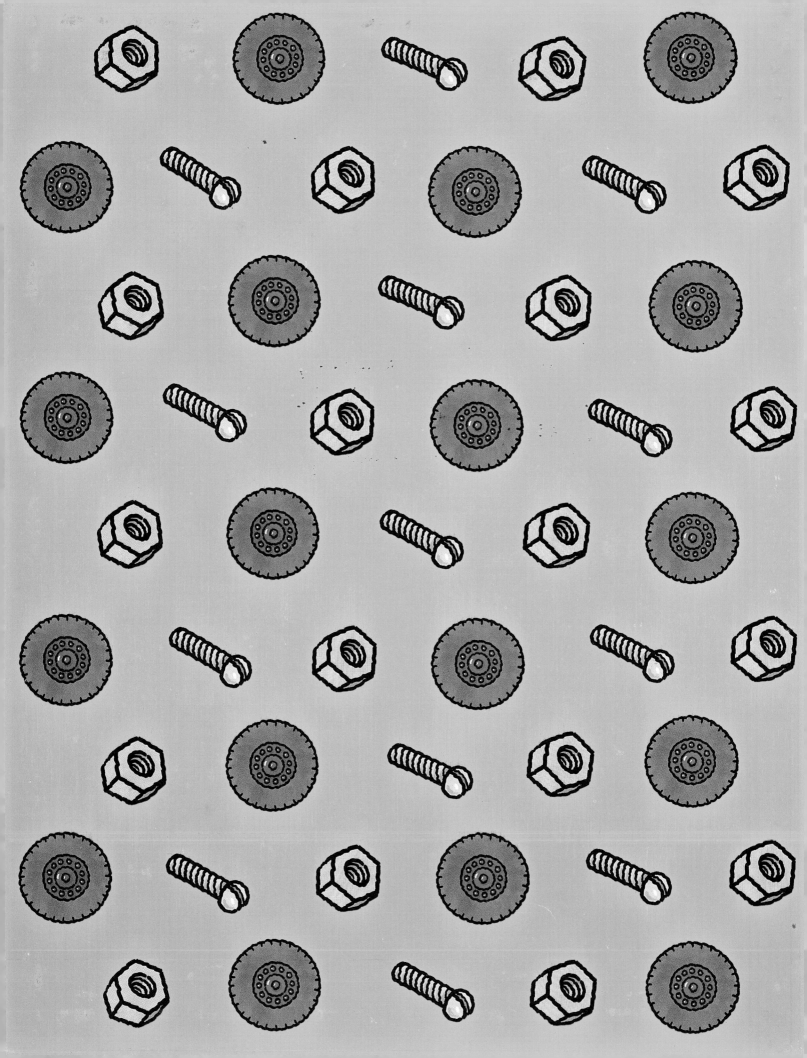